WildFlower Thoughts

ISHIL SIBAL

Copyright © Ishil Sibal 2025
All Rights Reserved.

ISBN
Hardcase 979-8-89906-820-1
Paperback 979-8-89724-590-1

This book has been published with all efforts taken to make the material error-free after the consent of the author. However, the author and the publisher do not assume and hereby disclaim any liability to any party for any loss, damage, or disruption caused by errors or omissions, whether such errors or omissions result from negligence, accident, or any other cause.

While every effort has been made to avoid any mistake or omission, this publication is being sold on the condition and understanding that neither the author nor the publishers or printers would be liable in any manner to any person by reason of any mistake or omission in this publication or for any action taken or omitted to be taken or advice rendered or accepted on the basis of this work. For any defect in printing or binding the publishers will be liable only to replace the defective copy by another copy of this work then available.

I would like to dedicate this book to the pressure of studies which made me procrastinate long enough to write this book.

Contents

Acknowledgments

I want to thank my friends Anya Rai, Anushree Ray, and Adwika Chaudhary among others for their constant support and my classmates who encouraged me.

I would like to thank my mother, Swati Sharma Sibal, for her unwavering patience and feedback during my writing and book publishing journey.

Thank you for always believing in me.

PART ONE

SHORT STORIES

1

The Banyan Tree

I

It was still raining hard when she looked up from the book of horror stories which she was reading. Suddenly she felt a dark shadow lingering outside the window pane. There was an absolute downpour, now, as if nature herself had sensed the ominous atmosphere. A chill seemed to be seeping through her nest of blankets.

The stray flash of lightning illuminated the world only to flee when the roar of thunder reached its ears. As it happened, the shadow outside her window seemed to be groaning and reaching closer, and closer, and…

Then she realized it was just The Banyan Tree, dancing in the wind, celebrating the rain, unaware of the fear it had caused her. Putting the book down on the bedside table, she decided it was enough ghost stories for the day. No doubt they would be the feature of her dreams, or rather, nightmares. So, she walked over to her window and watched the dance of the droplets, the sudden flash of lightning surely followed by a clap of thunder.

Despite the clouds being dark and there being no sign of life outside, the swaying of The Banyan Tree, its utter joy in receiving precious water, dripping down the leaves, even the clouds' lightning brought applause from the heavens. Like the dust on every surface, the rain washed away her fear.

II

And yet, and yet there was something wrong with the scene. She stared at it for what seemed like hours, but were only a handful of minutes. It was too peaceful, too… quiet.

Apart from the occasional boom of thunder, there was no sound to be heard. No pitter patter of the rain.

The swaying of the banyan tree now felt like a warning.

Suspicion wove its way through her spine. Fear began to press on her, eventually sinking its teeth into her flesh. The Peace in her heart spoiled to Unease. With the next clap of thunder, bumps dotted her arms.

Gathering her courage, she, with trembling hands, unlatched her window and pushed it open. A fresh wave of terror hit her. Not only was there no sound of the rain, but, instead of being greeted with wind on her face and the comforting fragrance of the wet earth, she stood frozen in the arid air, which made her tongue dry upon inhalation and the smell of burning, melting flesh…

III

Her eyes snapped open.

She lay there, face first in the soil, whose heat had made her feet blister mere hours after she had resumed walking. Dry soil jammed itself on her cracking lips, making them bleed. She didn't know when or why she fell. She suspected it had to do with the horrible pain grasping and tearing at her calves.

Her eyes were burning. She hadn't realized she had let them rest again. Her parched throat screamed for water. Her heart pounded in her chest, making its presence known, as if childing her for not having any fluids. But what could she do?

IV

She had stopped trying to call out for anyone left, she feared that she would cough up blood if she used her voice. She despaired at every drop of sweat that escaped her, every swallow of saliva, a reminder her that this thirst would not be quenched. Dehydration would have to be her cause of death. She shivered despite the heat.

Even her lungs were not spared, they were so tight it felt as if she was trying to inhale powder. Each breath dried her throat yet if she tried to hold her breath, a coughing fit would worsen her pounding head. The dire thirst drowned any feeling of hunger.

Her skin seemed only to be a paper covering over her body, going by the cuts her limbs were sustaining. Was it her imagination or was her blood darker than before? In an attempt to stand, she pushed herself up. Her arms shook and her legs protested under the strain of this simple manoeuvre. Black ringed her vision, her head felt like lead.

She stood up like a newborn colt and attempted to walk, she stumbled, managing only to worsen her headache. Her heart was trying its best to pound its way through its ribcage.

V

Perhaps… she could swallow the blood seeping out of her lip?

Blood is liquid. Water is a liquid.

She had never thought that she would ever attempt to drink her own blood as a substitute for water, but it isn't really the kind of thing one expects.

How old was she again? Quite a nice number she thought. The earth had no plants that were green, all were yellow or brown. Black slowly consumed her vision, as Insanity clawed its way to her defenceless mind. It seemed so funny that she cracked a smile. It wasn't autumn yet. Had they lost track of time? In her dehydrated, deranged mind she tried to go to the nearest yellowing plant, determined to ask. When really, she fell after a few steps.

She died there.

All that remained was the Insanity.

2

10th Birthday

Contrary to common belief, children do know when an adult is lying to them, not every time, but more times than adults anticipate.

The lies kids can see through, are small ones, like –

"Mom, are you are sure that this is the right answer?"

"Yes, I am sure!"

But the fact that she checks her phone the next instant – and starts typing on Google – is a dead giveaway.

Now this instance, proves both children's ability to detect lies as well as their intuition. As a bonus, almost any child, born between February to May, between the ages 7 and 14 in 2020 can relate to this, at least up to some point.

In advance, as I must warn you, this story shall be dramatic.

The reason for this is that, it is about a 9-year-old girl who just learned that her birthday got cancelled.

~ ~ ~

Her birthday, came after her father's, sibling's, and mother's birthdays. This was simply adding salt to the wound.

The father's birthday was celebrated quietly at home, as that was what he wanted.

The sibling who was a 4-year-old girl, celebrated her birthday in a Play zone in a mall. The four-year-old invited her friends, relatives and believe it not, her teacher.

The mother's birthday was celebrated by a three-day trip in a treehouse resort with just the four of them.

Then came the time for the 9-year old's birthday.

To begin banishing stereotypes; her birthday plans included no ponies, princesses, sparkles, or dolls. All she wanted to do was invite two of her friends (the very best ones) and go to a trampoline park.

This afore-mentioned Trampoline Park was quite famous and at a walking distance from her home, an ideal place, for both her parents and her friends.

It was all planned and finalized and agreed upon. Her plan was in motion, nothing could stop it.

Until, of course, everything shut down.

It was not on the last minute per say as she had her suspicions, but let us start where the story starts, or rather a bit before.

~ ~ ~

The point where the saga picks up is a mere few days after the mother's birthday. There was only a week left for the girl's birthday, a week where Anticipation awaited.

Unfortunately, Anticipation soon turned to Dread when all over the news came a certain COVID-19.

Well, in all fairness, the news was already everywhere during the time of the mother's birthday trip, but at that time, it was not affecting her.

Her suspicions only started when she heard that her birthday would get 're-scheduled' (read; postponed, or rather, as she felt, cancelled).

It was then, when she finally started to believe what her friends had told her about this new 'SARS-CoV-2'. Apparently, it was a new strain of an old virus which previously did not affect humans.

The more she heard, the less she cared about what this virus did to infected and started to wonder what it would do to her birthday.

Around this time, a temporary pre-lockdown/ voluntary public curfew had been placed into effect. This worsened her fears but, somehow made her cling harder to her hopes.

Deep down, she unexplainably knew that her birthday plans were cancelled forever. Schools were just scrambling and the world was thrown in a turmoil.

Yet, she simply could not accept the reality, thinking that this was just a bad dream.

She pushed all thoughts aside and focused on her day-to-day life. Unfortunately, she could not always keep the thoughts weaving the threads of hope for her birthday at bay.

~Five Days to her 10th Birthday~

She sat in the dining room where 15 minutes later her aunt was to arrive with her 5-year-old cousin. Everyone had made a big deal about her 10th birthday.

"Double Digits!" they said, "That is a huge deal, you'll be a big girl now!"

The poor girl propped on the highchair of expectations of her birthday, had a long hard fall to the ground of reality.

No one even broke it to her. So, she bumped and scraped and bruised herself on the way down.

Her Aunt arrived with her son. The girl's cousin was interested in things she was not. When she had expended all polite conversation that she knew, she started to engage in her aunt's conversation.

On hindsight, it was a terrible idea. The first few topics were not that bad, the usual, "How is school and studies," followed by "Oh, my dear, you look so thin, eat up!" Even when the aunt asked about her math skills, the girl was still amiable, polite, and appropriate.

But when the aunt asked, in a quite insensitive manner, about her birthday, she was nudged by the girl's mother.

Whispers exchanged.

Expressions changed.

The Aunt laughed it off by saying, "Well, its just one birthday!"

The irony was that she was one of those people who had told the girl that 10th birthdays are a big deal.

Also, it was more than one birthday that the girl lost due to the virus. This was just the beginning. The expression on the aunt's face, not the words was the thing that finally pushed the tears out of her eyes.

Thoroughly embarrassed for crying, she went to find an empty room where she could sulk in solitude.

~Four Days left to her 10th Birthday~

Her Aunt had left the previous day with her cousin after having dinner.

Fortunately, the topic of her birthday was not brought up again. It was primarily an uneventful day, unless one counts the commotion when her glasses were accidently left in a room, which was locked by her grandmother who had gone outside.

Honestly, the scene barely lasted 2 minutes before spare keys were found and her glasses retrieved. Later that day, her parents, sibling, and herself went back home so that they would not stay trapped in her grandmother's house.

~Three Days left to her 10th Birthday~

The girl, who foolishly still had expectations left, mostly thought about her friends. She was bored. There was no school at that point in time. All offices, malls, schools, markets were closed.

Anything that was not necessary was closed. The local grocery stores, plumbers, carpenters etc. were still in business.

That would, of course, change in a few days. The girl mostly sat in her room, looked out her window, and was lost in thoughts that day. Thoughts were only interrupted by breaks for food and minimal interaction and her chores.

~Two Days left to her 10th Birthday~

The girl's parents were debating whether or not to decorate the house and buy her a few more gifts as her friends would not be giving her any due to their inability to come. This meant that her Trampoline plan would not materialise and her birthday had indeed been cancelled?

This discussion was happening away from the girl's ears. She would, as she always did, find out about it sooner or later, or as in this case, the very next day.

Her parents ultimately decided in favour of their idea after weighing in the pros and cons of it.

Even with this, their last effort, taking in the gravity of the current situation, the girl, who was merely 9 years old, and had recently seen her nuclear families' birthdays celebrated according to their wishes, was bound to feel at least a pang of envy.

~One Day left to her 10th Birthday~

She woke up, determined not to be excited for the following day. Here was the thing, first came her father's birthday, then, exactly a week later, came her sibling's birthday. After a 25-day gap, came her mother's birthday. 16 days later came her birthday.

Seeing that a year has 365 days, their birthdays were in quick succession. This put sanitizer to her already salted wound, so to speak.

On top of that, her parents gave her the worst gift in this scenario, even though it was not necessarily a bad thing.

Hope.

They came to her room on that eve, she had been playing with her sister.

Her parents, came unaware of the effect it would have on their daughter, told her that she was getting a celebration.

BA-BOOM.
BA-BOOM.
BA-BOOM.

Was this true? Was it really happening?

They then continued by saying they were sorry but she could not go to the Trampoline Park with her friends and she fell further.

They explained that they would decorate the house by putting balloons of her favourite colours, along with alphabet balloons saying HAPPY BIRTHDAY followed by her name pasted on the wall of their living room.

In addition, she would get 10 gifts to symbolise her 10th birthday along with a cake. Though the bakery shops had closed, a lady in their apartment complex baked well.

She forced herself to look happy and excited – "Don't be selfish! I need to be grateful."

It was true that they were giving a lesser celebration, but it was also true that she was doing a crime by being disappointed by someone's best efforts.

"But everyone else got to celebrate THEIR birthdays, why can't she…?" She cut herself off, "…this inner monologue was not needed, even so, there is mom's brother, his birthday will also not be celebrated, and he is not complaining." What she counted off, that he was an adult and she was a child.

And adults don't really take birthdays as seriously as children do.

~Her 10th Birthday~

All and any resolutions for not getting excited dissolved when she woke up. For a moment, everything seemed perfect. But then she remembered that despite her mitigation attempts, the virus had, indeed infected her birthday plans and there was no cure for it.

Even with this dampening her spirits, she was still brimming with enough excitement, to open her eyes with a smile on her face. One can only do so much to a 9- sorry, 10-year old's birthday bliss.

But, for some peculiar reason, she did not want to get out of bed and go outside jumping.

It was almost like she was feeling dread for something. She had forgotten something, she was sure of it, so she tried to remember, and remember she did. The memories of yesterday came back. Her spirits, surprisingly, fell.

Determined to make her parents feel that they had done enough, because they had, she was going to put on her 'happy mask.'

She was getting 10 gifts. That was not a small number. There are people who can't even get one. So, she commanded herself to go through her morning chores, changed and went to her parent to wake them up.

What do you expect, Reader?

It is her birthday, of course she would wake up early.

~ ~ ~

The balloons particularly the alphabet balloons, were nice, only she remembers that her name was first to go. That was the work of her four-year old sister, who just wanted the golden balloons. The balloons of her name were the only ones within her sibling's reach.

About the cake, well, she tried hard not be upset. She had gotten a cake after all, why did it matter, if her sister blew the candles?

Her sibling was small, she was big, so she just had to deal with it like a good big sister, because her younger sister could not understand. That is why she had to let her sister blow the candles and cut the cake and have the birthday song sung for her. Even after her birthday had just gone by.

It should not matter, that her sibling got gifts on her birthday, even though she did not get any on her sibling's birthday because her sibling was small and even so, she would not mind, she would not let herself mind.

She needed to be a good elder sister. "I really should not care, if my little sibling is using my gifts, even if she is allowed to break them. If she ever did break my toys, she would never do it on purpose, and so, I need not be feeling bad."

"…and so, I need not feel bad" - she made this her moto. At least, for the next few years.

And so, started the global pandemic of 2020.

She survived.

But she was never the same again.

3

A Cat's Night Time Adventures

My human was upon the bed, napping.

Foolish human, could not even nap correctly. It was the moon which was in the sky, with his glitter sprinkled across the sky. I landed on the couch and began to hunt for the infernal sphere.

"Aha! There you are!"

I tensed, adjusted my posture, and…

Around fifteen minutes later, I had glorious returned victorious from the Infernal sphere. It had not stood a chance. Alas the rise of the glowing sun would revive the sphere and the fight would continue!

Something had moved. I jumped down and went to check on that food-giving-worshipper of mine. The human had turned, and a foot was dangling off the sleeping couch.

A foot.

No cat is fully convinced that the foot is the human. It seemed to me that my human used its foot to move, albeit extremely ungracefully. But when the foot was not in use and simply…

It had moved. That was it, and I pounced on the back-stabbing foot my human kept.

My human woke up (finally, human did not even stir when I entered or exited the room, which is not being particularly alert) and looked at me, finally opening its weak eyes, I had to say it was not… The foot made a counter attack, Ah! It was getting real now!

Apparently, the human liked its foot. It was beyond me why the human wanted to keep the foot. It was clearly an unreliable little flesh-bag (I could now confirm this statement, having been the one to draw blood). The human had escorted me out of its room and closed the door. Oh well, it was human's loss that I would refrain from protecting it from its foot. And there was absolutely…

I spotted it.

My arch nemesis; the rattling bird.

The little feathered immortal being was inedible and an enemy. Our battles have been legendary, and this one would not be an exception. Onto war, I thought and sneaked up behind the rattle bird.

PART TWO

POEMS

Hope

I have days yet to live,
I have challenges yet to face,
I have pages yet to write,
I have songs yet to sing.
I have mountains yet to climb.
I have time yet to spend.
I have friends yet to make,
I have years yet to grow.
I have books yet to read,
I have sights yet to see.
I have places yet to be.
My life is worth living,
I will live it fully.
If I cut my finger on a thorn,
A rose is yet to be seen.

The Corner

Promises are meant to be kept
She kept her promises.
The ones that mattered
She feels oddly detached, somehow
Sitting there near her Shrine, her corner
Trying to find a shred of comfort from it
It doesn't stop the tears shed.
No, seeing it only shows herself.
The only person she loathes
The only one she is unforgiving towards
Is it truly fair?
So many care for her
She cares not for herself, but for
Those around her
To believe that all those care
Play a façade waiting to be dropped
Fear of so much
Feels as though the weight of the world
Is on her shoulders
It pushes her to play nice and keep up as eternal mask.
The mask that binds her tongue is old, so old she fears to
discard it,
For who has the truly seen her face?

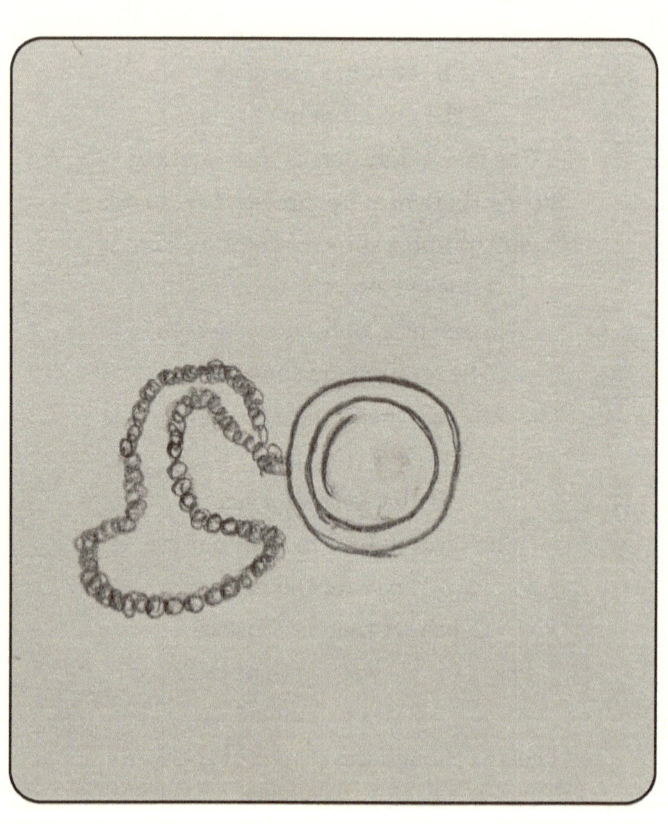

Observations

A student's life is governed
By a few things:
The subject, the teacher, the mood of said teacher,
fellow students and finally study
Fellow students carry an
Impressive amount of drama
The subject is subject to change
Along with the mood of the teacher
Study for most is pure grind-work
Although, stupidly sacrificing social skills
Proves to be harmful in
Almost every way possible.
I doubt that this is poem
But then, what would
Classify as one?

Figures of Speech

Any semblance of sense
That could be carried
Through this poem
Should not be seen seriously
The entirety of this experiment of expression,
Is an adept alliterated anarchy.
How I hope to humour this hunch
Is beyond me
I seem to be succeeding simply by sitting
What word would one work with?
This impressive impulse of imagination
Is indeed an indication
Perhaps painting a point
Plain perspective cannot place.

The End

Conclusions

I

Conclusions are a thing of curiosity
You spend pages Making a Point
Only to summarise it in a few lines
If you can put your point through
In so little,
Then why write so much?

II

I shall answer my own question and say,
A conclusion need not be a summary
It could end your writing.
In a way, that makes it stay
In the minds of the ones reading.

III

Hence concluding my confusion
On conclusions
I close this clause of my poems.

Nocturnal

The dark night sky is soothing.
When the world is at rest and
Sounds all slumber
When the moon washes us with its gentle light
When the trees finally take a breath of relief
That is the reign of dreams
When waves of sleep swish around your eyes
And the moon draws around itself the clouds
When the sky's eyes twinkle with the promise of a new
day ahead,
That is the reign of dreams.
The owls and bats come out of hiding
and the cats leap gracefully into action
that is the time when the sun sleeps
That is the reign of dreams.

Fall

And so I fall.
That's how I fall every time
I can't admit that someone I love
could ever be so wrong
Even if they are right
And so I don't feel
Because my feelings,
scare them.
I am unravelled
why can't I fix myself?
why can't I help myself?
How am I able to put myself in other's shoes,
If I don't have any of my own?
Maybe that is how and why I do it
To keep my cold feet warm
I don't have shoes you can put on
Because I am always in others'
My Shoes got lost and I didn't bother to find them
Because I was in someone else's shoes
I made a mistake then.
A lot of time has passed, and I think,
Now that my shoes are old and filthy
I am not really sure if they even fit any more
Because I changed

Do I find new shoes or do I walk barefoot?
Could I even bear the walk?
If I walk on enough thorns,
Placed in quick succession and closely together
Will I even feel anything at all?
Or will I feel so much that,
I fall?

Houses; Changes; Handwritings

I think I lost my ability to cry
And I'm not really sure why,
no matter how hard I try
My handwriting never seems right.
I really should stop being so
Dramatic
My work,
why do I always format it?
Well that was random.
I have exam tomorrow, I'm not sure I've studied enough.
Why must things always change?
In less than three weeks
I could be sitting in a new house
For, I have not a home
No person
No place
No thing
Could ever bring
the feeling of home for me
For they shall be snatched from me.
I know that thinking such is bad mentality

But isn't it a reality?
Don't wait for to me to see
Because, I will never truly believe
For that the happen to me
Thus said, you would be waiting for eternity

* * *

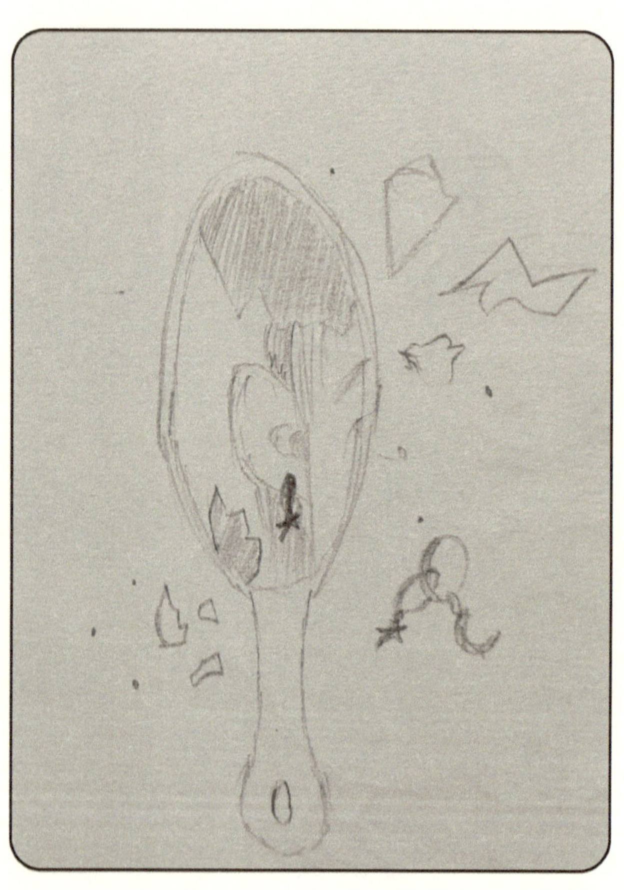

Nothing of Value

I

I am a complicated person, am I?
Double-edged doesn't even begin to cut it.
with due consideration, I am more of fragmented glass.
That's what I am
Scattered.
As people view me in various lights; shades; colours
Those who see the prism are few.
Three, maybe two.
And I know that most who know me
Think that it must be them.

II

Illusions fool the eye more than people think
Truth is almost never acquired when you blink.
Search long and search with your heart
Thinking reveals the ugly truth
But people like pretty
And lies are about as pretty as you get

III

As people ask why I wore
different earrings on each ear.

I only give them a knowing look
Knowing, all on their own, they'll cook a story up
When really, I just mixed up the pairs at home.
They think, therefore I become.

IV

The less you answer and
make seem common to know
The less they ask
It maintains the friendship
Yet gives away no new information.
There comes a point where all known about you is merely
made-up.
You've neither accepted nor denied it
But people believe it.

V

No one asks anything of you anymore
As they think they know all there is to know
But what do they know?
Nothing of value.

The Stairway to the Terrace

The stairway to the terrace was a thrill,
A thrill of fresh air,
of the sun of the day and stars of night
or the taste of rain or the wind on her face or in her hair

The stairway to the terrace was an old childhood friend,
whose memories she wrote anew with each day's end.
The stairway to the terrace was an escape
from the harsh world,
Its pretty lies
and harsher truths,
with words that cut like shards of glass.

The stairway to the terrace was an emotion
with its narrow steps.
And a roof without railing
where so many childhood nights had been spent.

The stairway to the terrace was waiting
Waiting for her light footfalls
going up towards an open sky
and see the clouds passing by.

To be Free

I stare in awe as the thunder rumbles
In the sky
Vibrating beneath my feet.
How the protruding light from
the clouds seem normal to me
I see and the downpour from a door of net
and of balcony cage in front of me.
I wonder how it would be if there was a
glass window in front of me.
No longer would I smell the earth
or hear the rain or feel the breeze
But,
I would be able to see,
More clearly, my friend, the tree waving
I would observe each droplet, and
their journey from the clouds above
to the ground beneath.
If I remove the glasses through which,
I view the world, would I be able to
see it more clearly?
How, I wonder, do the people who can
be in the rain, feel?
Happier than me, maybe.
Perhaps,

few don't realize.
Some,
Who like me think they are free
do not see,
how free they were meant to be
My friend, the tree waves to me.
Sways and rejoices to truly be free.
Free of the forces that control me.

Burnt Out

Nothing much is left say
I just... don't know
Anything, anything at all
take that in any way you wish
Can't find a flow
Stumbling, about to fall
but I'm okay... ish?
Life; a mess
I don't know why I'm writing this.
Though I can I guess –
I wish to glow
or bask in life's bliss.
But I Can't
Because I miss
the point
of all this.

Start

The irony of starting something is
time does not wait,
age does not wait.
There is no wait.
You've already started
what is left to do is
view the journey
and make most of what you do
There is no stopping
Only slowing down
Perhaps not as much as anticipated,
but progress is always there
Start;
There is no end to what can be achieved.

Worth of Words

I am unable to see, even if
Said to my face
how my words
could move someone.
It is a far-fetched wish
as I express myself in ink
so that someone may understand
even it is in the far future
It is the only reason I would wish
to be remembered.
A wish that somewhere, sometime, someone
could just get it
So that this hope
May give them hope.

Modern Beauty

Beauty is a bemusing concept
how does when one identify it
when the criteria constantly changing,
who even defines these parameters
that only a percentage of the population may possess
while all others run over themselves
to work their body into the latest
"ideal" box.
and their mind suffers more than their muscles
as one constantly beats oneself down.
Truly,
What better torture than one
that is willingly or unwillingly self-inflected?

Unenergized Empath

I feel as though, I am losing my empathy
I don't have the energy
to feel bad for you.
I understand your problem
but I don't want to help
Because my help is hypocritical
and usually ends up creating a mess
Yet you still come to me
Is this a flaw of humanity?
I feel as though you are draining my energy.
Latching on to me like a Leech
while I starve for a speck of comfort
That I know I will not get
It is tantalizingly easy, telling.
But you won't see my signs
and keep a good pace
of burdening me with your whines.
Sitting there, were you in my place
you would have simply walked away.
I feel as though I am taken for granted
a shoulder so to weep
a silent supportive, figure at your side

A *little pet* you keep
I think it would change should I just share
But I would have to stop feeling for your problems
to feel for mine.

Schrödinger

I

Time feels fluid
Days stretch like rubber
Yet months zip by like a jet...
The current moments feel so long
but ends so fast.
An hour of study; An hour of music.
The difference practically proves the Theory of Relativity
If time is not standard from atom to atom, then what is?

II

In the vastness where of space
Where even light has to fight
To get from here to there,
What a strange little speck we are,
Speculating whether a cat is dead or alive
in a box where we cannot see it
and we say curiosity killed the cat
When so many more humans have died due to it
Besides,
how can you say the cat is truly dead,
Isn't that the paradox of it?

SAVE
TREES:

Of Paper and Pens

My hand hurts
I'm now fully convinced that
Writing Exams is a scam
Did you know homework was invented as a punishment
Which implies,
All students are bad;
even those who complete the assignment.
Why waste paper and write with pens?
Do you how many pages I've filled,
Writing speeches, debates, paragraphs and declamations
about saving trees?
Hence, testament to how many trees are cut to make
paper,
We should ban school notebooks and test sheets.

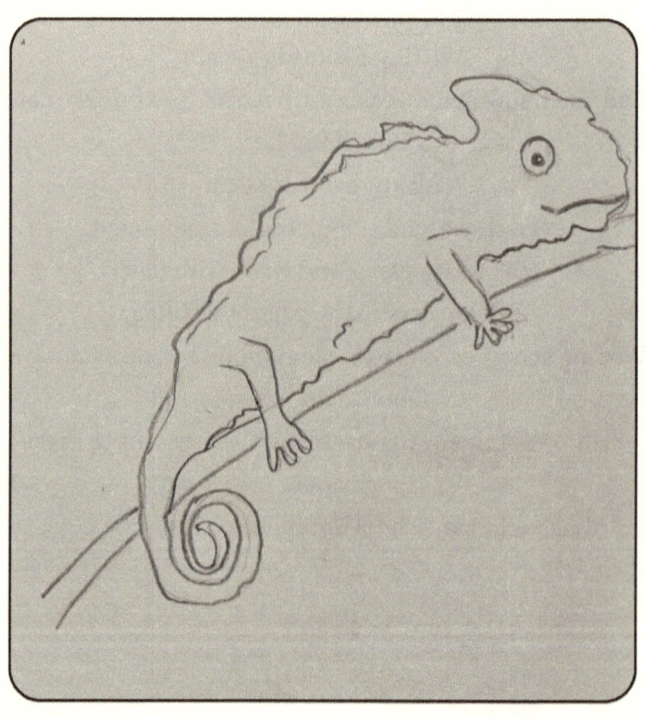

On Adapting

I

Sometimes I think I adapt too quickly.
It scares me
Do I truly adapt or do I simply
Learn to ignore the need?
How much pain will it take for me
to say something to somebody?
I'm not glad of the answer I get.
How much pain will it take me take myself seriously?
I know I have it in me to hold sympathy.
Then why can't I hold it for me?
Is adaptive even an adept adjective to describe me,
Or is it simply me strengthening the dam I've built
to suppress the flood of feelings that would inevitably
engulf me?

II

Next to none of my friends have seen me cry
I think, I've lost the ability
to even attempt to vent
I try but my comfort hinders me
and I lack the bravery.

Wants and Wishes

I want to do a lot of things
Can I do everything I want?
Or are my most my wants wishes, not needs?
That begs the question what needs are
At first glance; food, water, shelter, clothing
But then, what of health, wealth, education, and social
interaction?
Anything may be a need.
One might argue,
only food and water are enough,
if we live like nomads.
Another might just say that
Life is pointless
and there are no needs if
one willing to die
Need is a tricky word
It changes meaning when one changes their views on life
A need is everything between a whim and a base necessity
As one keeps justifying why they simply need what they
want,
It often transcends to the level of greed.

April Thesis

I

How does one express oneself
if one feels there is nothing to express?
Simply allowing oneself to speak
does not seem to appeal to me

II

How does one define trust
Does trusting someone
entail that they will trust me?
Is it feeling or an action,
Or is it action upon feeling,
the act of giving a desired reaction

III

Am I simply adding this verse
Because the number three means
something to me?
I cannot seem to write,
in anything but riddles, questions, and rhymes.
Does it say much about *me*,
or the *people* around me?

Trees

There is something so soothing
in a great leafy tree
shades of green glinting in the sun
Swaying branches in the breeze.
Sparkling leaves in the rain
Trees call to me
They sway and wave
To beckon me closer
Their roots, holding firmly
To the ground,
their branches
Reaching to the skies
Giving home to so many
Giving us air to breath
Giving us shade from the sun's rays
Trees stand tall before wind, storm and disaster.
They were here before us and they will stay until after

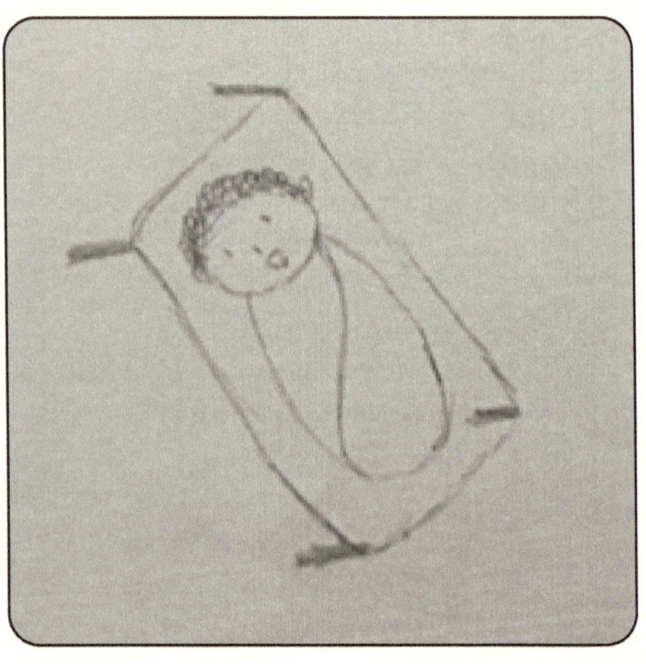

Memories

Before one's first step or word,
Prior to any fault or deed,
One is titled when one is born.
Do we grow up to fit our name
or
Does the Is the name change meaning to fit us?
Is the name an unfulfilled aspiration of the past,
or
is it a hope for the ones after us?
Do our Memories shape us,
or
is it on how we shape them?
Can the interpretation of different experiences
have the same outcome?

Art of Expression

I wish for people to understand the nuance in my words
Specifying small scenarios
That this specific specimen may not even see
Shattering the subtle sway of my words
Leaving confusion in its wake
Isn't that the beauty of words?
The interpretation of the individual that they interact
with.

Can I truly leave enough room between lines
That my expression of emotions is enough
And it is not so personal that others wouldn't understand
What is language but an excuse of intonation
What is writing but an escape from expression?

As soon as I know what to express the words scatter in
the dark of my mind.
Fluttering, flying past
making their presence known
but not to be seen or captured
Only to exist in my whirlwind of a head
It's not enunciation that I lack
its trust.

Still, I scramble to somehow show someone how I feel.
Counterintuitive and counterproductive.
Context clues and reading faces
only get you so far
in the art of communication.

•••

Isolation

I

It seems something is wrong with me; I am acting weird
and stubborn
there is a fuzzy ball of sad in my chest,
that sometimes gets enough static electricity for a strike
of sharp anger.
my posture seems defeated,
but my tongue sharp with shards carried in this hurricane
of emotion

II

What is going on here? Has rational me lost her mind?
to feel like a kid who can't control her tongue and has to
watch
With grim fascination at the dominos falling
it's not enough, it seems for me to lose my own mind, no,
it seems that I wish to drag others along with me as well

III

The negative in m is seeping out like radioactive waste,
damaging and unravelling everything
I wish to fling things at the wall to see them shatter
and then step on the shards of my doing

IV

I want to watch my bare feet bleed
for the crime of having no shoes of their own
I wish to let the cold, cold marble seep
into my cold feet to spur them into action of agony
Maybe then there will be fire in me.

V

If I go away from the people I love
then, at least they won't be hurt
but I sit here looking as though I could care less
while inside I try to sort out this mess

It Just Does

I

Life feels fake. It just does
I don't have the energy to write what I wish to say
let alone actually speak it
I barely have enough energy to think it
in the end,
I am left, half-heartedly grasping
at the strings of my mind
Trying to untangle my own feelings
it is some cruel irony, I think
for strings of others to be simpler to untangle
while I become unravelled
trying to wrap my head around itself,
Whenever I try to follow my strings
I wonder,
who manipulates my ever-tangled strings,
who makes me move through
the unending chore that is life
and onwards towards tomorrow

II

This feels dark. It just does
even though it really isn't
they're silly things, these strings
until you figure out how to pull them
and make grotesque figures, that were never meant to be
and wonder,
Is this who you wanted to be?

www.ingramcontent.com/pod-product-compliance
Lightning Source LLC
Chambersburg PA
CBHW022035150726
47990CB00002B/967